S0-ADS-339

THE CIRCUS
IS COMING!
Dedicated to Henry

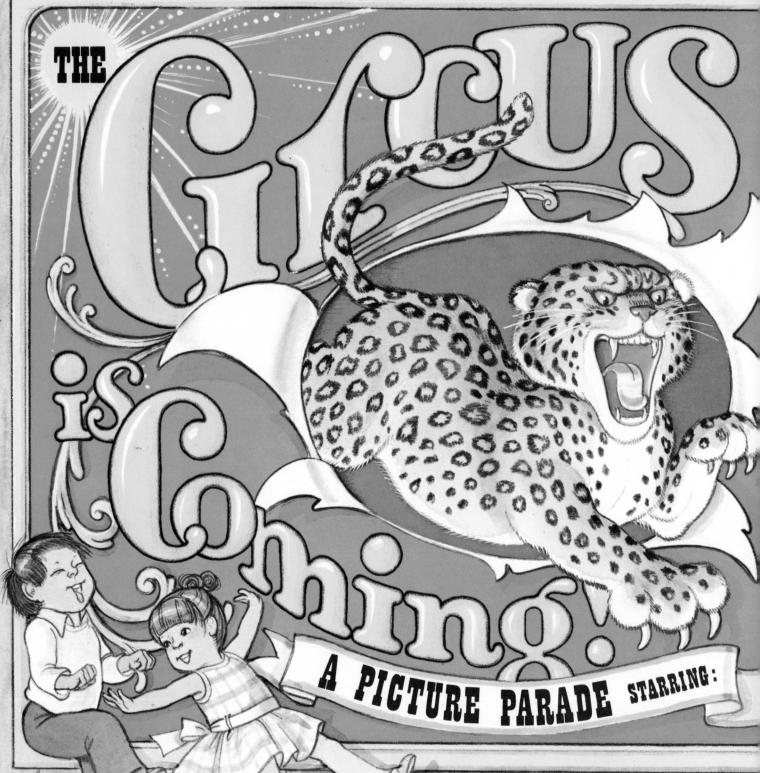

THE CIRCUS is Coming!

A PICTURE PARADE STARRING:

Golden Press • New York

Western Publishing Company, Inc.
Racine, Wisconsin

PROGRAMME

1. The Band Wagon: A Brass Blast-Off!
2. Fearless Felines: Tabbies and Tigers
3. A Cabload of Clown Cutups
4. Thrilling Teeterboard & Tightrope Tricks
5. Heidi, Hans & Helga's High-Stepping Horses
6. Outrageous Orangutans: A Courtly Caper
7. The Tumbling Ting-Tong Troupe
8. Pirate Pranks: A Clown Cannonball Hits . . .
9. . . . the Floating Island of Lost Treasure
10. The Wild Horsemen of Turkmenistan
11. Darling's Dogs: Cunning Canine Clowns
12. Star-Studded Spectaculars
13. The Glorious Garden of Delights
14. A Polar Paradise of Penguins & Seals
15. Chimpanzees on the High Trapeze
16. America: When the West Was Wild
17. Bumbling Basketball Buffoonery
18. An Exotic African Caravan
19. Peerless Performing Pachyderms
20. Finale: Fine Feathered Friends

240 Performers In 20 Scenes

BY HILARY KNIGHT

PARADE
TODAY!
COME ONE
COME
ALL
ABSOLUTELY FREE

Copyright © 1978 by Western Publishing Company, Inc. All rights reserved.
No part of this book may be reproduced or copied in any form without
written permission from the publisher. Printed in the U.S.A.
GOLDEN®, A GOLDEN BOOK® and GOLDEN PRESS® are trademarks of Western Publishing Company, Inc.
Library of Congress Catalog Card Number: 78-68425

BAND
WAGON

Snarling and spitting tigers make me shiver.

But cats can be gentle, too.

How do so many clowns fit in that taxi?

Whirling, twirling on fingers and toes,

I laugh so hard my sides hurt.

KING
NEPTUNE'S

*Treasure
Isle*

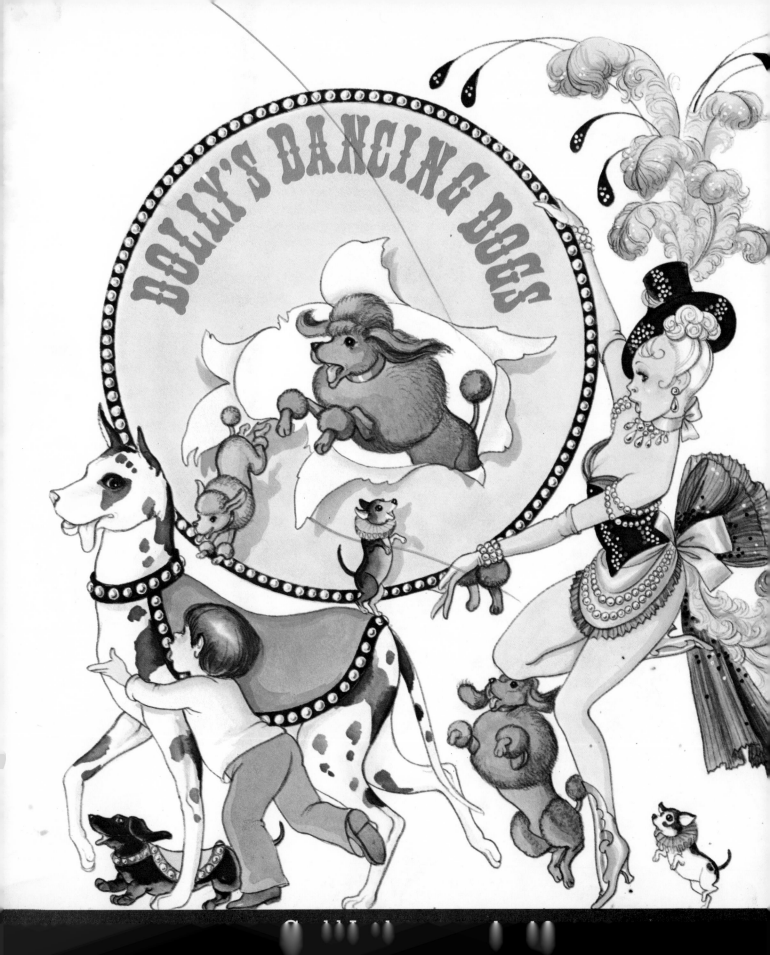

Big dogs, little dogs, prancing dogs . . .

My, what interesting people.

RENALDO RUBBERMAN

SALOME SERPENTINA

INNIE ATURA & WEE MAC

. . . and Eskimos and penguins and furry seal babies.

"Come on, children," says the stiltman.